Whooping cranes breed in Canada then fly thousands of miles south to Texas for the winter. In 1939 there were only 30 left in the world. Since then they have been carefully protected and their numbers are gradually increasing.

Birds of paradise used to be shot so that their beautiful feathers could be used to decorate hats and clothes. Now they are in danger because their jungle homes are being destroyed.

It is a shame when an animal species vanishes for ever. Sadly, more animals are in danger now than ever before.

Some animals are killed for their skins or feathers. Elephants are shot for their ivory tusks, rhinos for their horns. Elephants and rhinos are protected by law, but poachers are still killing them.

Lemurs, like the indris and the strange little aye-aye, live in the jungles of Madagascar. Their numbers are decreasing because their jungle homes are being destroyed by farmers.

Pollution is another threat to animals. Fish are poisoned when chemicals from factories and farms get into rivers. Birds and otters soon die if they are coated with oil spilt by a tanker.

The addax and oryx are rare desert antelopes. You can tell them apart by their horns; the addax's are curly, the oryx's are straight. Nearly all of these antelope have been hunted by man.

Addax live in Africa. They gather in small herds and wander over the desert looking for grass.

Oryx once lived in Arabia. They are now extinct in the wild, but some have survived in zoos and reserves.

Before Europeans arrived in North America, huge herds of bison roamed the grass plains. Then hunters started killing them with guns. Not long ago only a few hundred were left. Now they are protected and numbers are increasing again.

Green turtles are threatened by hunting and egg collecting. They lay their eggs in holes on deserted tropical beaches, then cover them with sand and return to the sea. Egg collectors find the nests by poking the sand with sticks.

Now the turtles' nest sites are being disturbed by tourists. Bright lights from new hotels and resorts attract the baby turtles when they hatch. Really, they should be going in the opposite direction – towards the faint glow of the sea. Many die in this way.

Crocodiles and alligators are hunted for their skins to make shoes and handbags. The biggest ones live in Asia and Australia but they are becoming very rare.

American alligators were in danger due to hunting and because their swamp-land homes were being drained. Now they are protected and numbers are increasing.

Like many jungle animals, gorillas, chimpanzees and orangutans are in danger. Their forest homes are being chopped down and burned by farmers and road builders.

Mountain gorillas live in families in rain forests in Africa. There are only a few hundred left. Sometimes they are killed by poachers.

Orangutans live alone – eating leaves and fruit high in the jungle trees. Young ones used to be captured and taken to zoos but most of them died on the way.

Chimpanzees are very intelligent animals. They live in family groups called troops. They are also in danger because their homes are slowly being destroyed. Young chimpanzees are also taken from the wild to be used in experiments.

Some people put animals in danger by hunting them or by polluting their food and water – but many other people are working hard to save animals.

But perhaps the biggest threat to wild animals is the destruction of their homes. Without their natural habitat, many species will not survive.

Many countries now have nature parks where animals can be better protected. In China the few remaining wild giant pandas live undisturbed in the bamboo forests.

Some very rare animals, like the Hawaiian goose and Przewalski's horse, have been bred in zoos and are being returned to the wild.

Many governments have now made laws against selling rare animals or their skins and feathers, or tusks and horns.

A lot of work has to be done if endangered animals are to be saved. For without their natural surroundings, there may come a time when all of the animals in this book can only live safely in zoos and nature parks.

Endangered Animals Quiz.

All the animals on this page are in danger. Can you decide why? Look back in the book for ideas if you get stuck.

1. Osprey

2. Snow leopard

3. Gavial

4. Three toed sloth

5. Golden lion tamarin

6. Right whale

7. Chinese egret

8. Sable antelope

Answers

1. Pollution poisons its food.
2. Hunters kill it for its fur.
3. Hunters kill it for its skin.
4. Its jungle home is being destroyed.
5. Its jungle home is being destroyed.
6. Whalers kill it with harpoons.
7. Hunters kill it for its feathers.
8. Hunters kill it for its horns.

Lions are getting rarer, too. Most of them live in nature parks in Africa.

Big cats used to be hunted for their beautiful fur. Tiger skins were made into rugs. Skins from leopards, jaguars and cheetahs were made into fur coats. Most people now agree that a big cat's fur looks better on the cats than it does on people!

Pollution kills birds like falcons and eagles. Farmers spray their crops with poisons to kill insect pests. If a falcon eats animals that have swallowed the poison, its eggs may not hatch. In America, bald eagles are poisoned by eating fish from polluted rivers.

There are only about two thousand tigers left in the world. They are dangerous animals. They kill goats and cattle and sometimes they become man-eaters.

It is difficult to find room for tigers to live safely alongside people. Nature parks are the only places where they might survive.

In the past few years dolphins have slowly disappeared from around our coasts. Dolphins are not fish, they are mammals like dogs and cats. They must come to the surface to breathe. Each year thousands are caught in fishermens' nets and drown. Pollution in their food may be making them have fewer babies as well.

Edited by Belinda Gallagher
Cover design by Oxprint Ltd.

ISBN 0 86112 720 X

Published by Brimax Books Ltd, Newmarket, England 1991.
Printed in Hong Kong.

LEARN ABOUT

Endangered Animals

Great whales like the blue whale and the bowhead whale used to be much more common than they are today. But whalers have killed so many with their harpoons that some species have nearly disappeared.

In one year, thirty thousand blue whales were killed. There are now only a few thousand left. Most countries have banned whale hunting. But blue whales are still in danger because there are so few left to breed.

The dinosaurs became extinct 65 million years ago. No one really knows why. Perhaps the weather became too cold for them to survive.

Mammoths were woolly elephants. They became extinct about ten thousand years ago. They were killed by hunters for their meat and skins.

When all the animals of one species die, the animal becomes extinct. This means that it will never be seen again on Earth.

The dodo was a flightless bird. It had no enemies except man. It could not fly, so it was easy to catch for food. The last one was killed about two hundred years ago.

In North America, millions of passenger pigeons were shot by the first settlers from Europe. The last one died in a zoo in 1914.

LEARN ABOUT

Endangered Animals

Written by Jane and David Glover
Illustrated by Brian Watson

Brimax · Newmarket · England